How You Can Have it All

Even if You Think It's Impossible

By:

Matt Maddix

Featuring:

Caleb Maddix

Book Cover Design: Ryan O'Donnell

Edited by: Amy Kochek

Printing and/or ordering information: amazon.com

Table of Contents

CHAPTER ONE

Change or Die

After hours on the flight from the Philippines to Canada, I finally arrived at my destination. I can't really describe the heaviness that I felt because it consumed every aspect of my life. I was physically, emotionally, and spiritually drained. After seven speaking engagements in a row, countless hours spent traveling, and with very little rest, I settled into my hotel to prepare for my next event. As my limp body sat barely erect on the edge of the bed, I turned to my two friends who were traveling with me and said, "Guys, something is not right. I don't feel well at all." Their response was encouraging and simple. They told me to take some medication and lay down for a minute. I only had a short time until I was to speak, so I lay down and tried to sleep it off.

As soon as the back of my head hit the pillow, I began to feel my throat swell up. Thinking it was only my imagination; I shot back up and attempted to swallow. Pain shot through my body as fear simultaneously gripped me. I became genuinely afraid for my life because I didn't know what was happening to my body. Speaking and moving my mouth became painful, so I told my friends to go to the event without me while I stayed back to get some rest.

The sound of the door clicking shut seemed to echo through the room. Once again, it is hard to describe the moments that followed because I had never experienced this before. In that moment I felt as though a thick, dark cloud of loneliness came into the room and suffocated me. I tried to sleep off these overwhelming emotions that were causing physical and emotional pain. It was as if my body had been on overdrive and the silence invited a voice that my busy-ness had quieted for months. The thoughts came in waves. I was trying to figure out how to slow down my schedule, how to make time for my son, how to calm my regrets, and how to forgive and heal. The thoughts and pain didn't subside, but my absolute exhaustion allowed my body to finally surrender to sleep.

It was pitch black and my mouth was open as wide as my body would allow while I tried to suck in air. During my few short hours of sleep, my throat had swollen more until it was nearly closed all the way. I was gasping for air and that same fear gripped me again. Only this time, it was met with panic. I quickly dialed 911 and was rushed to the ER. Once I entered the hospital, they didn't even need to do an initial diagnosis. The condition of my internal body that had been breaking down for years was now on physical display for the whole world to see. I had done well hiding it for quite some time, but I could not run from it now.

After the doctor worked on me, he gave me a moment to gather myself. I sat up on the table and he looked directly at me. He said one of the most chilling statements to me that still brings tears to my eyes. "Mr. Maddix, you are a very lucky man. You have been given a second chance at life. If you would have waited 30 more minutes, you would have been dead." In that moment, I didn't think about my business, money I've earned, places I've traveled, or the people I've taught through hundreds of speaking events. In that moment, all I could think about was my son's precious face. Caleb, this innocent young boy, would grow up without the love, guidance, and affirmation of his dad.

It may sound cliché to say that my life changed in that moment, but it really did. Standing face to face with your mortality ignites an indescribable passion for change. When I left the hospital that next day, I knew that my life would never be the same and it hasn't been.

I am so passionate about any topic dealing with families because I almost lost mine through my own choices. Friends, I don't care what level of success you experience. You may have more money than you have ever imagined, enjoy an extravagant lifestyle, or run a lucrative business; but if your family, health, or finances is failing, then you are failing.

At what I believed to be the height of my career, I was traveling all over the world speaking to thousands of people and changing the world. I made incredibly good money, ate at some of the world's finest restaurants, and had reached a high level of fame and notoriety.

By the standard of society, I was doing some great things in this world since most of what I did involved investing in people and doing missions work. All of these actions should have equaled a successful and fulfilled life. But there was another side to this success.

I was in my 30s, 40 lbs. overweight, exhausted, stressed, irritable, depressed, sluggish, and absent from my life as a dad. I assumed that my son, Caleb, would be fine with my long hours of work and the days away from home because I was a, "good dad."

Months went by without exercise while I filled my body with pizza, junk food, and sugar. I didn't get proper sleep or rest. During this time period, I went to the ER twice because my family thought I was having a heart attack. All of these should have been warning signs that a change must occur, but I just excused it with the belief that every successful person has to make sacrifices. The only problem with this mentality is that I was sacrificing my life for supposed success. I was no longer willing to do that.

I had to make some drastic decisions in order to change my life. That moment of my transformation brought to memory a hospital visit I made years before this incident to see my precious grandfather. My family and I were pretty shook up after he suffered a massive heart attack. I'll never forget the look of fear in his eyes as he gazed at the doctor and asked, "Doctor, am I going to survive?" The doctor met my grandfather's stare and void of emotion he replied, "No, you are not going to survive."

The gasps of shock filled the room as the gravity of this news impacted my family. A moment of silence followed while my grandfather tried to register this devastating revelation.

The doctor's voice interrupted our disturbed silence. He turned around and said, "Mr. Maddix, I got a question for you. Do you want to live?" My grandfather quickly replied, "Yes, sir. I want to live." The doctor then said, "Well, I see people in here everyday with heart attacks and heart failure. Despite the danger of their condition, not too long after they leave the hospital they are back to their old habits. They aren't eating right, exercising, or getting the proper rest. You know what, Mr. Maddix? If you are serious about living I have three words for you. Change or die."

Those words pierced through me like swords. However, at the time I was young and foolishly thought that nothing like that would ever happen to me. That's usually what we all think. We pity tragic moments but allow them to pass without doing any self-reflection. I left the hospital that day intrigued by the doctor's words but unwilling to take the steps to change.

Years later, those words still resonated inside of me, but now I was ready to do the work so that, "change or die" would transform from mere information to application. My change or die moment was the greatest blessing that I've ever received because on that day, I chose to change and I've never looked back.

CHAPTER TWO

A Kid's Perspective

My dad was scheduled to go on yet another trip. It had become normal for me to wave goodbye to him as he boarded countless planes or finished loading up his car. In this instance, I was holding his hand as he approached the gate in order to get ready to board his plane. In my other hand, I held on tightly to a piece of paper in hopes of giving it to my dad before he left. The night before, I was sitting in my room crying because I knew that he was going to leave again. I *hated* those moments. I understood that part of his job required him to travel, but at the age of 4, I didn't know how to accept the fact that my dad was gone a lot.

While I was sitting on my bed, I decided that I was going to draw him a picture. I don't remember the exact thoughts that went through my mind when I drew it, but I knew that I was hurting. On one side of the picture, I drew myself. I was standing with my arms reaching in the other direction with tears streaming down my face. On the other side of the picture stood my dad whose back was turned towards me as he boarded a plane.

The phrase, "A picture is worth a thousand words," definitely applies here because my picture spoke to where I was at the time. I was a little boy who needed his dad. Most of my earliest and best memories involve my dad, and he was and still is my hero. When he traveled, he would come home and make sure that he was 100% engaged in his time with me.

He spent time mentoring, coaching, reading, and instilling an overall positive mindset. My dad was a great dad, but he was gone so much that he began to miss out on special moments in my life. I remember when I started playing baseball and the excitement I would get when I knew my dad was going to be able to make it to one of my games. On the flip side, I remember the extreme disappointment I would feel if he was out of town for a game.

When my dad was away and my mom was unable to watch me, I would spend that time with babysitters. This happened a lot, and I hated it. I just wanted my dad to be home. Finally, to my surprise, he did come home – and he stayed home. Once again, I was young so I don't remember specific details; I just remember that I was able to see my dad everyday. It was like my prayers had been answered.

The bond we shared seemed to strengthen when my dad decided to stay home. We spent weekends together, he was at every one of my baseball games, he was there to pick me up from school, and a day did not go by that I did not see him. Those years are filled with countless memories and lessons I learned from him. My dad has always been my number one teacher and supporter.

Because of his decision to stay home and fully invest in my life, I have achieved great success as a 14 year old. I'm an entrepreneur, speaker, and author. The exposure I receive allows me to meet a wide variety of people. From that, I have had a few individuals say that the only reason why I am successful is because of my dad. I don't hesitate to wholeheartedly agree with this statement. Who I am today and the success I've earned is directly connected to the daily investment my dad made into my life.

I am forever thankful that he made the sacrifice to leave a job that took him away from home in order to spend more time with me. It was truly a risk and one that could have hurt him financially. However, I've watched my dad build a business from the ground up, earn more money than he's ever made, and become the best dad in the world all at the same time. I can honestly say that my dad has it all and because of this, I have it all too.

I want to pause and talk directly to the parents that are reading this book right now. Many times, parents believe that merely providing financially and supplying a constant stream of things will satisfy you children. I'm here to tell you that it doesn't matter how many thousands of dollars you pour into games, clothes, and electronics, it will never replace the quality time that your children are yearning for. My dad always told me that kids spell love, TIME and I agree with that statement.

When my dad was traveling, I didn't go hungry and we were not poor by any means. Toys and games surrounded me while my parents were absent. You see, it doesn't matter how many cars, yachts, and houses that you own. It doesn't matter how much you buy your kids. At the end of the day, your kids want YOU. They want your time, your affection, your affirmation, and your love.

I have vivid memories of the time I spent with my babysitter. It wasn't that I hated her; it was the fact that I hated feeling abandoned.

Listen, parents, I know that some of you are working hard and you want the best for your kids, but trust me, the best is YOU. You are better than any amount of money, trip, or tangible extravagance that you could ever give your kid.

I don't know what my life would look like now if my dad had continued down the path he was headed. It is quite possible that he would have been dead by now, or even worse, he would be alive physically but our relationship would be emotionally dead.

I know that I don't speak for the minority, but I am the voice of the majority. Kids NEED their parents and your decision to make the necessary sacrifices in order to invest in their lives will determine their overall success or failure. I hope that you make the decision to invest because there is another Caleb out there who is waiting to change the world. He just needs a parent that will shape him into the world changer that is inside of him. Will that parent be you? Is that child your son or daughter?

My dad and I are here to help you answer those questions. Continue reading to discover how we can connect with you and your family to help you replicate the success we have found in our own relationship. It is not a fluke; rather, it is a repeatable process that if done correctly, will give you the results you desire.

CHAPTER THREE

Are You Ready For Change?

My journey to get to where I am has not been easy, but it has been worth it. Here is one of the most gratifying parts of my journey towards incredible change. I realized that it is indeed possible to be successful in business, my health, my home, and my spirituality at the same time. I don't have to choose. I can have it all. No, seriously, I really do have it all. I'm not just saying this to sell you a gimmick or motivate you. I'm telling you this so that you can relieve the mountain of stress off of your shoulders.

See, people ask me all the time why I'm so passionate about life. They see my insane focus on my health, the value I place on my spirituality, and the fierce way I protect my quality time with my son, and they always question the source of my motivation. The answer is steeped in so much emotion that I get choked up even thinking about it. Friends, I sat there when the doctor told my grandfather to change or die. I've been in the emergency room twice with what they thought were heart attacks. As I stated earlier, I also had my own near death experience. In addition to this, I watched 4 of my closest friends on earth tragically pass away from heart attacks due to neglecting their health.

I attended each one of these funerals as the families agonized at the unimaginable loss. In one instance, a child of my deceased friend had to be pried off the casket as he screamed, "Daddy, please don't leave me."

You see my friend, that's how serious this is. You only have one short life. If you crash your car tomorrow, you can buy another one. If your house burns down, you can find somewhere else to live. But you only get ONE short life, and that is why you must absolutely determine right now as you are reading this book that no matter what price you have to pay or sacrifice you have to make, you will change or die.

At this moment, some of you may still be thinking the same way I was when I heard those words in my grandfather's hospital room. You may be moved, but at the back of your mind you are thinking that it is not going to happen to you. The thought may center on the fact that you're still young and you have time. You know what, you may be right. It might not happen to you. The span of your life may be even longer than what you believe it will be.

Guys, here is the truth. I would crawl on broken glass to plead with every person on this planet to please do whatever it takes to become the best version of you. Don't let your pride or ego get in the way of the necessary changes that you need to make. Your kids, spouse, co-worker, family members, and friends deserve a complete and whole individual.

So now, I need to turn my attention to you – my friend. That's right. I may not know your name, background, or current life's condition, but I do know one thing has connected us today. You want to know how to have it all. In fact, you may be so burdened by life, that even your success in business feels like a burden. I want to help you today, and I believe that what you are about to read and embark upon will literally change your life. Before we start, I want to tell you whom this book is for so you don't feel like I'm wasting your time.

This is for:

1. Goal oriented families who are passionate about health and success.

2. Families that want a healthier relationship but are struggling to find time to have it all.

3. Families that are committed to personal growth and have a "whatever it takes" attitude.

4. Married or single parents who are overwhelmed and never feel like they have any "me" time.

5. Families that love each other but struggle to communicate and spend quality time together.

6. Broken families that are ready for healing and change so that they can have peace and harmony.

If you fall into even one of these categories, then you have picked up the right book. For years, I have worked with families who were struggling to connect and find success in every area of their life and I can tell you that it is possible to turn your family around if you follow some simple steps.

In fact, I'm believing that you will have success in your family, health, spirituality AND business. Don't believe me? By the time you are done reading this book, I'm going to prove it to you that:

1. You can have massive success in business or career without neglecting your health, even if it seems impossible right now.

2. You can spend more quality time with your family without feeling guilty about work that still needs to be done.

3. You can live with the deepest levels of peace, get more rest, take more vacations, and have more energy while still being extremely productive at work.

4. You can create an atmosphere in your home where your children feel confident, comfortable and safe.

5. You can do all of this without feeling like you are wasting time, losing money, or neglecting people who depend on you to deliver product.

I know this may sound unbelievable and even impossible, but if you follow me along this journey, I will take you step by step through the process. I believe in this process so much because I personally used it and have seen my life and my son's life completely transform. So this is what I want you to do first. I want you to eliminate all distractions that are surrounding you. Turn off the TV, put your phone on silent, close your computer, and go to a quiet place where you can relax and put 100% focus on you.

Ok, let's get started. In the pursuit of balance between family and business, I know that a good deal of people struggle with the feelings of guilt. They feel guilty or frustrated because they haven't been able to spend quality time with their family, workout, eat healthy, or have the time to do the things they really love and want to do. I understand this feeling, folks because this was my life. For some of us, that guilt we feel causes jealousy of other people who are having the life we really want, and we become envious. To avoid those emotions, we work even harder while burning ourselves out. Then, hopelessness sets in. We feel like we can't have a healthy body, time for ourselves, or the energy to spend time with our family. And for some of you, you may feel like it's too late and you've made so many mistakes that you cannot turn it all around.

Well, I've got great news for you. It is NEVER too late to change. Remember, you have to make the choice. Change or die. No, your death may not be a physical one. In fact, you may live for many more years to come. But what sort of life will you be living? You may show all signs of physical life, but all other aspects of your life categorize you as the walking dead. The keys to an abundant life are at your very fingertips. You just have to choose to pick them up, put the key in the door, and turn it. Notice, that all of those steps require action. It's not enough just to know that the keys exist, you must use them.

One of the biggest complaints that I hear from parents and families is that there is just not enough time in the day to focus on their business and family. Before we move forward I want to get rid of this myth because you do have time. The real problem is what you are doing with this time. This was an eye opener for me because I realized that I had to optimize the time I had in order to activate change. This is when I decided to make some shifts in my life.

This is going to be an important word from here on out because there are three shifts that must occur in your life in order for you to have it all. These shifts will cause you to have more peace and success in every area of your life to include spiritual, health, business, and family. You will be able to have success in your career without gaining weight or neglecting your family.

Balancing your work schedule will bring more time for you to play and enjoy life. Exercise, eating healthy, and an increase in energy will be normal for you. Also, you will be able to go on more family vacations, get more rest, and create more family traditions. Most importantly, you will be able to experience clarity of mind and have more time for yourself. It would be a definite tragedy if you spent your entire life giving and adding value to the lives of others while yours slowly crumbles.

There are four essential elements to success, which include financial, spiritual, family, and health. When one of these is not functioning properly, it can completely disrupt your equilibrium. Think about how your car operates. If one of the tires is low or completely flat, it inhibits your vehicle from functioning properly. The same can be said for the balance of your life. Ensuring the highest level of performance in all of those areas means that you can have it all.

CHAPTER FOUR

Refocus

B efore we start with the first shift, I would like you to get out a pen and do an exercise with me that will allow us to be more successful in this process. I would like you to make a list of things that you have done right and a list of things that you have done wrong. Before we move forward, it is important to establish where we currently are. Let me make this clear. There is no shame in where you are. We all have issues and regrets, but the difference between you and everyone else is that you have picked up this book and made the decision to make a change. I celebrate and applaud you for your bravery. Now, jot down as many things as you can in a journal or notebook answering these two questions:

1. What Have I Done Right?

2. What Have I Done Wrong?

I hope that you were able to see a snippet of your life through your rights and wrongs. It is interesting that many times people can easily identify what they have done wrong, but when they are asked to articulate what they have done right, they struggle. Both your rights and your wrongs have brought you to this pivotal moment, so we are not going to dwell on either of them; rather, we are going to use them as a foundation to rebuild.

With that being stated, let's move on to our first shift:

Refocus:

Without realizing it, our lives can begin to go off course until we find ourselves in an unrecognizable place that we never wanted to be in. To avoid continuing down a destructive path, we must determine where we want to go. We must be specific and detailed otherwise we will allow circumstances to dictate our lives. You must be clear about what you want for your life. I'm going to list some prompts below so that we can establish what you really want from your life. With that information, we can continue to shift. Use your journal or notebook to answer these questions.

1. If you could live life 100% on your terms, what would it look like?

2. Next, I want you to clarify your values and non-negotiables. In other words, what are the things and people that you value the

most. What would you die for? I want you to make a list of your values.

3. Now that you have made personal declarations concerning your life, I want you to make a list of what you want your family to be known for? Also, make another list indicating what you would like your legacy to be?

In order to become your best you need focus, commitment, and massive action. We've made the decision, but now we must use action and be committed to follow through. The decision part of this shift is very important, but the most important part is your commitment. When I made this shift in my life, the first thing I established was that my number one value was my son. Similarly, I wanted to be known as the best dad in the world. From the point of my decision, I began to take actions so that these statements went beyond words and became a reality. I had to make some changes so that I could live my values.

I'll give you a little snippet of this list I made that shifted my life into focus.

- 1 year without traveling away from Caleb

- After a year, only travel 4 nights a month

- See Caleb everyday. If I'm away, I will send a video

- Every Friday, 100 cups of Starbucks to the homeless and a special breakfast with Caleb

- Turn off my phone after school until bed time

- Write a letter to Caleb everyday

- Lots of laughter and memories

- Master being in the moment

- Start serving the poor weekly

- Never miss any of Caleb's baseball games

The action I took based on this list completely changed my life and my son's life. What I didn't realize is how significantly my decision would impact the quality of my son's life and mine. The results were unbelievable. Below are some of the successes that he has achieved.

- Wrote his first book by age 12

- Interviewed on National TV – 8 Million Views

- Featured in FORBES

- Featured in Huffington Post

- Featured on Fox News

- Featured in Entrepreneur Magazine

- Founder of "Kids 4 Success"

- Earned $100,000 by age 14

- Over 85 speaking requests across the world

- 111,000+ people on Facebook fan page

- 4 viral videos got over 2.9 Million Views

I made the decision, made the commitment, and got clear about my life and look at the results that it has produced. How many of you would like to see these types of results? As a dad, I am extremely proud of what my son has accomplished. However, outside of every speaking engagement, financial success, or public notoriety, I am most proud of my son's developing character. He is mannerly, respectful, extremely focused with his life, and well balanced. I don't have to worry about my son hanging around the wrong people, getting into drugs, or being rebellious and disrespectful.

Even though I'm so honored with every success and personal growth that I see in him, there will never be anything that will compare to the relationship that we share. My relationship with my son is truly amazing and is one which parents and kids envy because we have such a special bond. The strength of this relationship only came when I made the decision to refocus my life.

Similarly, Caleb's belief that I am the greatest dad in the world means more to me than any accomplishment I could ever earn in my lifetime. He respects, trusts, and honors me as his dad. We enjoy an enriching relationship filled with positive energy, quality time, and unconditional love. My friends, no award, accomplishment, or amount of success will ever compare to the fulfillment of strong family relationships.

My challenge to you is to be the best in every area of your life. Be the best physically, spiritually, in your family, and in your business. Go all in so you can have it all

Before you can get the results and be the best, you must be brutally honest with yourself. You must ask yourself these three questions:

1. What do I need to KEEP doing?

2. What do I need to STOP doing?

3. What do I need to START doing?

Completing this exercise was a game changer for me because it literally created an outline for my next moves. It brought perspective to the habits and choices of my life. I'll give you a portion of my lists so it will help guide your own.

Keep Doing:

- Laughing

- Think Positive

- Pursue growth

- Inspire others

- Love unconditionally

Stop doing:

- Drinking Coke and Soda

- Eating Sugar

- Eating Fast Food

- Being away from home more than 4 days a month

- Not living off of a budget

- Living without a schedule

Start Doing:

- Juicing raw fruits and vegetables

- Eating clean every 3 hours

- Drink water and green tea

- Spend time with Caleb everyday

- Budget

- Live off of a daily schedule

The answers to these questions are so essential so that you can regain focus and ensure that your values and non negotiables are either what you are going to keep doing or what you are going to start doing. Also, you need to take a close look at what you need to stop doing because many times, these habits or choices determine the overall success of our life. To better assist us in this stage of our refocus, I want you to fill out your list using those three questions to guide you. Once again, it is important that you are as detailed and specific as possible for this exercise.

** **TIP:** You may need to get away for a day in order to be truly clear on these answers. Perhaps choose a time of day that you are not as busy and your mind is clear.

1. **What do I need to KEEP doing?**

2. **What do I need to STOP doing?**

3. **What do I need to START doing?**

Now that you have completed this exercise, I want to warn you that mastering this shift will not be easy. Many times when speakers or authors tell you about their achievements, they don't give you the whole story accompanied with practical steps to replicate the process. Obviously, I can't tell you my whole story in this book, but if you continue down this journey with me by reading my upcoming books and taking my courses, I think you will be able to get the whole story.

In order to get as practical and transparent as possible in regards to this first shift, I'm going to tell you that refocusing is difficult, and it will cost you something.

I do a great deal of breakthrough coaching calls with single parents, and during one of my calls a parent asked me how in the world I was able to be successful in business and still have quality time with my son. The best answer I can give is that I became one of the most radically focused human beings on the planet. In fact, I don't believe anyone can really have it all until they master the art of focus. What did this mean? Being practical with you, this meant that I had to say, "No" 90% of the time.

This little word, "No" had more pushback than I anticipated. It upset friends and caused them to distance themselves from me because I had to place strict boundaries on my time and priorities.

Here is the reality. Your friends and family are going to struggle with you living a focused life because of the strict order that is required to stay balanced spiritually, physically, relationally and financially. Listen, you are going to have to say, "No" without apologies. That is literally what I did. I said, "No" 9 out of 10 times. I implemented boundaries and strictly protected my time. This didn't come without adversity. People were frustrated because the nature of my life completely changed. My decision to focus meant going to less ball games, removing long meaningless conversations from my life, and narrowing my recreational time with family and friends.

This does not mean that I don't have a social life or that I don't go out with friends or family. It just means that I am more intentional and strategic with my free time. These were some of the sacrifices that I had to make so that I could shift my focus to my business and my son. Obviously, the pay off was and still is worth it.

It can be the same for you, too. There is always a pay off when you live a focused life. It requires discipline and a mental toughness to not worry or fear what other people think about you. You have to be able to deal with the looks of disappointment, negative remarks, or passive aggressive comments. Whatever their responses are, you have to maintain a laser focus. A person who lives a focused life is willing to sacrifice momentary pleasure because they can see the eternal value of their focus. They are big picture thinkers, and that is what you have to become.

I personally know fathers who play softball 4 times a week. I don't understand this. If you have kids and a business, you can't afford to spend that amount of time away from greater priorities. Let me make this clear. There is nothing wrong with having "me" time. In fact, you will learn in this book that "me" time is essential. However, radical focus dictates that your "me" time must be scheduled and balanced with the rest of your commitments, and it should never outweigh your greater priorities.

Refocusing is perhaps one of the most important shifts that you will make, and the success of the other two shifts will not occur unless you master this one. You can't go to greatness and get more done without focus. You can't succeed in business and with your family unless you are focused. You must have the ability to say no and the discipline to execute. Remember, say no to the good so you can say yes to the best.

Many people love the message of focus, but they do not like the grind and discipline it takes to live a focused lifestyle. Focus means that you wake up early so that you can get the job done and get home early to your family. It means that you avoid social media and ESPN so that you can make your sales calls. Focus requires that you go to the gym early in the morning even when you don't feel like it. Focus means that when you are with your kids, you turn your phone off and stay in the moment, and when it's time for you to be with your spouse, your entire being is in that moment.

Robby's Story:

Robby was VERY successful in business. He made a great deal of money and even owned his own suite at the Dallas Cowboys stadium. He is also one of the greatest human beings you will ever meet. At the same time, he was frustrated because he couldn't spend the time he needed with his family and he was 40lbs. overweight. Like many, he was at his breaking point.

I started doing one on one coaching with him and helped him get focused about his values and non-negotiables. I asked him what he wanted from his life. After establishing his non-negotiables and values, he got clear about what he wanted, lost 40 lbs., strengthened his relationship with his wife and children, and he's happier now than he has ever been before. Not only does Robby have success, but also he now has time to spend with his family and to exercise and take care of himself. He's finally in a place where he has it all in his health, business, spirituality and relationships.

CHAPTER FIVE

Restore

O ur first shift has allowed us to establish where we are and where we want to go. The second shift requires a little more digging.

Restore:

The concept of restoration is so encouraging because the message behind it is that it doesn't matter how bad you've done in the past, you can begin again. We all have regrets and decisions that have negatively impacted our lives and the lives of those we love. But that doesn't mean that we cannot take action in order to heal and restore relationships. The first step in restoration is to list all of your regrets in your journal. This is not to bring up uncomfortable memories; rather, this is a time for you to acknowledge your errors, feel the pain that is associated with them, and let them go. The last part is the key to restoration. You must let go of those regrets. Dwelling upon them only traps you in the prison of your past. Write them down, read them, feel them, and then close your eyes and choose to release them.

Many times, we wait until we mess up to start making changes. Regrets come after we have already made the mistake, but what if we could anticipate them before they occur? Think about how many pitfalls you could avoid if this was done. This was actually something that I incorporated during my restore shift. I thought about what I would regret at Caleb's 18th birthday. If you are a parent, I'm sure you can relate to the fact that our kids grow up so fast. Without realizing it, they will become adults and the precious moments we had with them will have been wasted if we are not intentional.

I wanted to avoid this, so I began to imagine Caleb's 18th birthday party. All of our friends and family were there, and Caleb was enjoying his moment. After the celebration, he came up to me and said, "Ok, Dad. I'm going to go out with my friends. I love you." Even typing these words gets me choked up because of what it represents.

I will always be Caleb's dad, but when he gets to a certain age, my level of involvement and influence will shift. Knowing that there are only a few short years I have with my son before he begins to embark upon his own life's journey, I knew that I needed to take some actions that would minimize any regret that I would have during the years I have with him. The first thing I did was to make a list of all the things I would regret at his 18th birthday, and I reversed regrets into actions.

Here is a list of what I would regret at his 18th Birthday:

- Missing out on his baseball games

- Being unable to see him grow everyday

- Not preparing Caleb for his future

- Not spending quality time with him

- Not keeping my word

- Caleb thinking I'm not the greatest human being in the world

- Not getting what he needed from me

- Not being trustworthy

- Not talking to me about things that matter

Since you have already released your regrets, I want you to engage in a similar activity that requires you to reverse potential regret. Think about your spirituality, family, career, and health. What are regrets that you may have 10 years from now concerning these areas listed above? Fill in those regrets in your journal:

Family   **Spirituality**

Health   **Career**

You have just taken some huge steps toward having it all, my friends. Restoration is available to all of those who seek it, and I know that each of you is on a journey towards restoring your life and the life of your family. However, I want to make sure that we are not dwelling in the graveyard of our regrets. We are moving forward. Let me share with you the 4 key steps to moving forward.

1. Ask for forgiveness from family, friends and yourself. Give a sincere, heartfelt apology.

2. Don't defend yourself or make excuses.

3. Forgive yourself and let it go.

4. Refuse to dwell on regrets by continually reliving them in your mind or conversations.

Over the years, I have learned that every experience, whether it is beneficial or hurtful, serves as a learning opportunity. We've already acknowledged our regrets and we have made a plan to minimize future regrets. Now I want you to look over your list and write some lessons that you have learned. This is a good reflective point that allows you to gain purpose from your mistakes.

I can only imagine the emotions that you are experiencing after making your list and even after reading this chapter. Some of you are just now realizing how much of an impact you have had on your family whether that is positive or negative. Perhaps you have identified that you neglected, disappointed, or hurt your family. Maybe you have crushed your spouse and your kids. You may be filled with regret feel right now.

All I can tell you guys is that I've been there. If I really let myself dwell on all my regrets, it could easily bring me to a place of tears, heartbreak, and sadness. This is what I want to say in response to these emotions. Our family really loves us, and if we lay aside our pride and stubbornness, we would realize that restoration is awaiting us. Before we get to the restoration point, we must make some things right, and in most cases, that begins with an apology.

We must look our families in the eyes and apologize for the mistakes we have made. Most relationships and conflicts could be healed with a simple apology, but most of us are too stubborn or prideful to do this. Sometimes being right isn't even worth it. You always win when you ere on the side of humility. Don't allow your "rightness" to rob you from years of peace with your family and friends. Commit to becoming an emotionally healthy person that doesn't get offended easily and accepts apologies. Whether you are the one who has been hurt or you have hurt others, decide to make it right. Holding on to these offenses can block current and future relationships. Apologize sincerely and as often as necessary.

It is so important that our apologies don't come with excuses or justifications. We must simply acknowledge our actions, take ownership of our choices, and sincerely apologize for them. It may sound something like this. "Listen, I owe you a complete apology. I was 100% wrong and I take full responsibility for my actions. I'm so sorry for neglecting this family, and I'm so sorry that I made you feel less important. I'm also sorry that I haven't given you the love that you deserve." A true apology requires humility, and especially for my male audience, it demands that we swallow our pride and simply own our errors.

Even after the apology, you cannot expect your family to open up automatically. Trust must be rebuilt, and that will come through patience and consistency. Don't get angry, defensive, or attack. Let them see the sincerity of your actions that follow the apology, and they will begin to respond to your remorse.

Not even God can change your past. It is forever over. Part of the restoration process is forgiving yourself and letting go of the guilt. Don't allow yourself to feel the emotion of guilt. Even though your family still might be hurting from the decisions that you made, live in the moment, let it go, and don't beat yourself up. Allow your family the space and time to heal while you take baby steps toward real change.

If you take this advice to heart and actually do it, it doesn't matter how devastated your family is, it can be healed and restored. Today is a new day for you to start over. Don't waste this opportunity or this moment. In fact, I encourage you to pause right here and take some time to self-reflect and make the necessary apologies that are needed. Trust me, when you make it right, you will immediately feel a burden being lifted and the restoration process will begin.

Joel's Story:

When I first met Joel, he was at his wit's end and frustrated. He reached out to me for coaching because he needed someone to hold him accountable and ask him the difficult questions that he needed to answer. His greatest struggle was in his relationship with his daughter and he wanted to improve it. At first, he blamed his ex-wife for poisoning his daughter and for his own daughter's perceived hypersensitivity. After going deeper with him, I helped him to realize that it was his uncontrolled anger and constant raised voice that was driving a wedge between him and his daughter.

I empathized with him because I knew what was like to experience frustration as a parent, but I emphasized the fact that it was his responsibility to maintain control over his reactions despite his emotions. I had an honest moment with Joel and told him that he was completely at fault for his disconnection with his daughter. I knew he would be shocked to hear this, but I told him that I would share the actions required to receive healing in his relationship with his daughter.

I instructed Joel to go to his daughter, get eye level with her, maintain a tender look, grab her hands and say, "I owe you the biggest apology and I want to tell you that I'm so sorry for the way that I reacted. When I raise my voice and scream, I know that it brings fear to you and I'm so sorry for causing this. It is my fault that you feel nervous and insecure when you are around me, and I want to ask for your forgiveness." I assured Joel that if he told his daughter that and then spent everyday trying to avoid any of the behaviors he apologized for, that he would begin to rebuild his daughter's trust. Eventually, their relationship would be restored if he was consistent.

Joel made sure to give his apology without excuses and embraced his daughter even though he knew she might pull away. I reassured him that even if the expected response was not there, he should still continue with his sincere apology.

After his apology, he invited his daughter on weekly dates and treated her like a queen. Per my instructions, Joel had his daughter make a list of the top 25 things she liked to do and every week he did something different. He was a gentleman and treated her the way that he wanted future men to treat her.

Months later, he reached out to me again and told me that he owed me his life. He said that his relationship with his daughter is stronger than it has ever been before and that they have a daddy daughter date every single week. He told me that he hasn't yelled at her since our coaching session and the trust between them increases daily.

Chapter Six

Relax

ow that we have done some necessary restoration, we can transition into the last shift. The final shift that will allow you to have it all is to relax.

Relax:

The word sounds easy enough, but most of us don't really know how to relax. We think that it involves sleeping, watching TV, or scrolling through our phones. Sometimes these passive activities do nothing but make us lethargic. Relaxing should bring you peace and tranquility that allows you to feel recharged.

Tip #1:

Make it a priority to relax and enjoy life. You may be unsure about what activities you could take part in that would cause you to relax. I will make a list of some below, and if you begin to incorporate these into your life, you will see an extreme difference in your level of stress and anxiety.

- Yoga

- Meditation

- Get Good Sleep

- Listen to Music

- Get a Massage

- Spend Time in Nature

- Journal

- Exercise

- Live in the Moment

- Have more sex

Tip #2:

Have a family fun night on a weekly basis. It is so vital for you to spend quality time with your family. The activities may vary, but set aside a specific time that involves purposeful activities. One thing that I did with Caleb was to create a family fun box. I bought a box of Ping-Pong balls and Caleb and I wrote fun activities that we could do together on the balls. Each week, I would have him pick a ball and we would do that activity. During our family nights, we would put our phones away, rid our minds of distractions and focus on each other. We created some amazing memories and have had the time of our lives together.

Here are some examples of activities that we put on the balls:

- Putt-putt golf

- Bowling

- Downtown bike ride

- Downtown Disney for dinner

- Night on the beach

- Game night at home

- Pizza and ice cream

- Go to the movies

- Family game night

Tip #3:

Go out of town and take more family vacations.

I am constantly surprised at how many families neglect vacations. There are so many excuses as to why they don't take them, but I'm telling you that it is worth the money and time. It is an investment into your family and your own sanity. They don't have to be extravagant trips and you don't have to go broke. Find an environment that will allow you to enjoy the sites and each other. When your on vacation make sure that you:

- Have fun

- Make memories

- Laugh a lot

- Start new traditions

- Unplug from business

- Don't talk about stressful topics

- Sleep in

- Get out of your routine

- Eat the HECK out of ice cream

- Take pictures and videos

- Don't argue and fight

- Sleep in

Caleb and I have literally been all over the world and created so many memories and traditions. Each year, we go to a cabin in Tennessee to relax and enjoy nature. We have been ice-skating in Central Park, four wheeling in Canada, and hiking in the Great Smokies. These moments are precious to me because they strengthened our bond with one another.

Here are a few ideas for family vacations:

- Cruise

- Camping

- Cabin

- Resort

- Family Success Retreat

Vacations are an opportunity for you to grow together as a family while you are relaxing. This is especially true with the Family Success Retreat. It is a weekend designed to give you and your family the tools that you need in order to succeed. There will be sessions with me and my son, Caleb, that will contain life-changing content, which will transform your family. At the same time, there will be numerous relaxing activities as well as family oriented outings that are meant to bring families together.

Friends, this is not a gimmick or a sales pitch. I am making more money now than I ever have in my life, but at the same time, I am more family focused than I have ever been as well. It IS possible! I am fulfilled in my relationship with my son, business, health, and spirituality. I have not had to sacrifice success for my son. I have found a way to maintain my focus on both and I found ultimate success.

I know that life is hard and there are so many pressures that we face everyday, especially for all of you parents out there. It is not easy raising children, maintaining a home, and going to work each day. Some of you have difficult bosses and stressful work environments. This can take a toll on your life. I can understand this because as a single parent, there are days when the pressure can get pretty intense, but I have determined to make my home a safe, fun place where I can go to relax and recharge.

Yes, we need to go on more vacations and find ways to escape the stressors of reality, but your home shouldn't be the source of your stress. That's what this book is about. I'm throwing you a life jacket to help you escape from this sea of life that seems to be sucking you in.

Take a moment to step back from your environment and determine what must change in order to make your home, work, and even you body a place of peace and relaxation. I want you to make a decision to make time now to meditate, focus on your gratitude, journal, enjoy sunsets, read a book, enjoy a movie, etc. I encourage you to do something that brings relaxation to your current mindset and alleviates the thick cloud of stress and negativity that may be surrounding your mind and heart.

My friends, I understand what it is like to be busy and stressed. I am involved in 8 different businesses and have 7 business partners. I travel the world, I'm a speaker, writer, consultant, and I'm raising a 14-year-old celebrity entrepreneur. In the midst of all of this, I consistently slow down in order to relax my mind and center my thoughts.

This is so key for you in the relaxation process. Some of your homes are filled with so much tension and stress that you have no place of safety. That can all change with a decision to relax. Slow down a little bit and remember that just because you slow down does not mean that you are neglecting your passions and work. It means that you understand the value of controlling and reclaiming your mind.

Let your home be a place filled with laughter and joy. Don't let your environment be an outlet for your underlying tension. It should be the happiest place on earth filled with peace. Parents, don't take life so seriously. Stop drowning in the stress. Come up for a big breath of fresh air and RELAX.

Malissa's Story:

Malissa had a secret smoking addiction and was consumed with fear-based thinking. She spent most of her time being afraid to make decisions and lived based on other people's opinions. All of her relationships were failing and her family was falling apart. She was battling with self-limiting beliefs, and she was tense because her life was not working for her. She was exhausted, frustrated and unfulfilled.

She reached out to me for help and after eight weeks of one on one coaching, her life completely changed. She hasn't smoked in 8 months and is living her life with complete peace and fulfillment. Malissa met her soul mate after 8 weeks of coaching with me and married him 4 months later. She is now pursuing her passion of becoming a certified life coach with Tony Robbins. Malissa followed the formula that we will be showing you in *Mentor with Maddix*. She now has it all – success in health, family, business and spirituality.

CHAPTER SEVEN

You Only Die Once

Years ago, I was stunned when I found out that my mentor, friend, and father figure passed away. Words cannot express the devastation and emptiness I felt at the news. Trying to navigate through those emotions was a difficult task because of all that this man had imparted into my life. The amazing part is that he lived his life investing into so many other people. He was an evangelical minister who preached some of the most profound messages, led thousands of people, and left a powerful legacy that spanned the entire world. By the Christian realm, he fulfilled his purpose and mission on earth.

I packed my bags and took the lengthy drive to the location of his funeral. The church was packed – standing room only. Thousands mourned the loss of this great man and I was among them. I wept through most of the ceremony. I knew that it would be a difficult moment for me, but I was blown away by the kind words that were shared about this phenomenal man. After the funeral, I gathered around some close friends and this man's son to share some memories. Nothing prepared me for the words that his son shared concerning his father.

He looked at the group standing in the circle and with a monotone voice and emotionless face he said, "I really didn't know my dad." Those words still send chills through my body. This man who made such a huge impact on the world and was a great family man somehow faltered in his relationship with his son. I don't know the exact details of his life or where the disconnect occurred, all I know is that at the moment of his death, he left behind a stranger that he called his son.

My mentor traveled the world for a large part of his life and spent countless hours in front of audiences and in one on one counseling sessions. During those many engagements, how many of his son's sports events did he miss, how many one on one chats with his son did he neglect, and how much quality time was forfeited to help someone else? One of the most important people in his life felt abandoned and lost. What a tragic story to have. Hearing this gave me an even greater push to continue making the changes in my life so that my son would never say those same words on the day of my funeral.

I hope this story gives you the same inspiration to make sure you are experiencing success in all areas of your life so that your story is different than the one I just told. I don't believe that his son's pain discounts the good that my mentor did in this world. However, I do believe it casts a shadow on his legacy because his first and foremost role in life was a father, and without careful consideration, he allowed gaps to exist in that role. Not only did he suffer, but also his son paid the ultimate price.

Also, I remember reading a fairly popular story about a father who took his son on a fishing trip. They seemed to have a wonderful time of connection and communication. Later on that night, the father and son started to journal the events of the day. In the father's journal he wrote, "I took the boy fishing today, and it was a wasted day." At the same time, the son wrote in his journal, "I went fishing with my dad today, and it was the greatest day of my life."

Many times, parents view the time they spend with their children in the same way this father does – as wasted time. They may feel like they could be doing other "important" stuff. It is amazing that what we view as a waste of time or unimportant can leave a lasting impact on our kids' lives. Parents spend so much time doing and making moves that they can miss the real connection and emotions of their kids. At the point of death, the only memories that your kids will have are the memories that you never made together.

It would be a tragedy if the truth of the failures of your life were not revealed until the day of your death. The unfortunate part of this is that by then, the truth will be irrelevant because it will be too late. This doesn't just involve the truth about your family. This can include your success, health, and spirituality. What if your death was directly caused by a health condition that was totally treatable through disciplined decisions to control your poor health habits? What if your multi-million dollar business idea went to the grave with you? What if you lived your life in fear and you refused to take the risks that would give you continual peace?

Life is too short and it moves so fast. The need for change is expedient and it awaits your response.

CHAPTER EIGHT

The People Trap

One of the most shocking revelations that I received through this transformation process to having it all was how many people disagreed with my decisions and vocalized their disapproval of me. It was as if people were more comfortable with me as a sick, tired, disconnected young man. My success began to make people feel uncomfortable and many tried to negatively classify me as radical or that I had "lost it." Initially, it was difficult for me to let some of these relationships go. Some people made it a bit easier since they cut me off first. However, due to the focus of my life and where I knew I wanted to go, I realized that I just could not take some people with me on my journey. Was it hard? Of course. Was it painful? Very much so. Was it necessary? Absolutely.

Getting caught in the need for approval or affirmation of others, or what I like to call the "people trap," will keep you at a place of stagnation and frustration. You need to embrace the fact that you are not going to be able to please everyone with your decisions and your life. It is a truth that you must accept in order to move forward.

This is where most of us get tripped up because we spend so much time trying to please everyone else. Before we make a move, we get feedback from so many people that everyone else's voice begins to silence our own intuition. My friends, if you don't stop doing this, you are going to wake up one day realizing that you are living somebody else's life. The job you choose will be influenced by someone else's opinions about your strengths and weaknesses. You will allow someone else to choose your spouse. Even the clothing you wear will be based on the opinions and advice of others.

This is the crazy part. The people that you trying to please probably won't even attend your funeral. And if they do, after the funeral is over, they will be in the kitchen downstairs at the funeral home eating fried chicken talking about something else besides you.

Here is the reality. This is YOUR life, and you are the only one that gets the opportunity to live it. So my question to you is, why are you allowing everyone else to dictate the type of life you are going to live? People that choose to pursue greatness and live out their purpose are unique. They don't fit into a crowd. The choices they make and the habits they insert into their lives seem strange to ordinary people. If greatness is what you desire, then stop trying to fit in when you aren't meant to.

If you say that you want to have it all and that you want to be great, then you must prepare yourself for the results. This means that you may not be able to spend time with the same people or be present in the same environments that you are used to. These two actions may be very hard for some of you because you have built your life around people. Some of you may even be chronic people pleasers. Let me speak directly to those people. You cannot have it all and please everyone at the same time. It is impossible.

My greatest breakthrough to having it all came when I stopped trying to please everybody and when I made a conscious choice to stop caring about what people said about me. I'm not a callous person by any means. I really love people and I cherish relationships, so I don't say this flippantly. It took a lot of tears, self-reflection, and healing to get to this place, but it was necessary.

This step of escaping the people trap is so essential to your journey of having it all. Those who are stuck are the ones who will never live life to the fullest and won't be able to have it all.

Here is the good news. For those of you who want to break out of the people trap, you get to live life on your terms. You get to choose to have it all! You don't have to ask for permission to live a balanced life filled with peace and contentment. And let me tell you, while there is great sacrifice involved, the joys that follow are innumerable. Unburden yourself with the expectations and opinions of others and decide today to live YOUR life without apologies or explanations so that you can have it all.

So, live! Go all in 24/7. Wake up early in the morning and work hard all day. When you are at work, work and when you are with your family, be with your family. Commit to excellence and become the best. Never settle for average in any area of your life. If you are a husband, be romantic, sexy, and fun. If you are a dad, be the friendly dad that plays and the one that is there at the ball games cheering on your kids. If you are a wife, be supportive of your husband's dreams. If you are a mom be funny, involved, and listen to your kids.

Make all the money in the world. Make a bucket list and accomplish it. Be a man and woman on a mission. Be bold and courageous. Become the greatest version of yourself and leave a legacy that will impact generations to come. Live with integrity and serve those who are in need. Don't wait until you retire to do what you want. Follow your passion NOW!

CHAPTER NINE

Message from My Heart

As I near the end of this book, I find myself at a deep moment of contemplation. During one of my recent writing sessions, my prevailing thoughts were how much money I was going to make on this book. I was thinking of the social status that this book might bring. I asked myself, "Will it become a New York Times Bestseller and shoot me into a realm of extreme notoriety? Will this book be on the Oprah show? I know that might be a little too blunt for some of you, but I am not afraid of my truth.

In the midst of these thoughts, the only real thing that was burning in my soul and that my heart was beating for was the images of millions of parents that are hurting and fighting so hard to break through in their lives. I know that all of you want to be a good mother or a good father. I am aware that it is your desire to be successful but not at the cost of your family and personal sanity. That is why I wrote this book with such passion, conviction and emotion.

I wrote this book with the 10-year-old boy in mind whose dad hasn't taken him fishing or gone to any of his games because his dad was busy trying to find himself. I also wrote this book with the dad in mind who hasn't healed from his own experience as a neglected son. This book is also for those who may be trapped by the idea of success. You may be trying to keep up with a lifestyle you built when your business was expanding but now face extreme hardships due to the economy.

The content of this book meets each of you at different points in your life, so I don't know exactly where all of you are at this point. One thing I do know is that all of you want more. The problem may be that you are in a place that may leave you feeling overwhelmed and hopeless.

This is where I must tell you a piece of my story that I have yet to share. When I made the decision to change or die, my life didn't automatically begin to transform miraculously. I faced some extremely difficult times. Part of my having it all meant that for 2 years I lived at poverty level. Caleb and I lived in a Sunday school room and while living there, my truck was repossessed. It was by far one of the most embarrassing and demoralizing moments of my life. Here I was, the mighty Matt Maddix - the man of charisma and passion who literally spoke to 17,000 people at one time. I led movements, made and lost millions of dollars, traveled the world, and experienced great fame. However, in my decision to have it all, I had to lose it all. Everything that I thought mattered and I believed defined me was gone in what seemed like an instant.

I don't know what your journey is going to be, and I'm not saying that you are going to lose it all. I am saying that after my near death experience, I realized that my son was the only thing that really mattered. Because of this, everything that I lost did not devastate my life. It actually had the opposite effect. It fueled my passion to finally live. You see my friends, Caleb would rather have his dad living with him in a Sunday school classroom than living in a mansion without his father.

Shortly after leaving the classroom, I lived in an alley in the back of some guy's house in this horrible neighborhood. Then, a few months later, I stayed in somebody's garage for 6 months. During this time, I was finally able to save enough money to rent a small one bedroom apartment. Caleb stayed in the bedroom and I slept in the living room. I remember those nights quite vividly.

Of course those years definitely served to humble me, but I didn't care because my son had a dad. I was able to live my passion and do what I love, which was to spend quality time with my son. I tell people this all the time. Rich people have money and wealthy people have time. While I may not have had a great deal of money during that time period, I felt like the wealthiest man alive.

The essence of this book is not based on theory or something from Google; rather, it is rooted in my real life experiences. I know I've said this before, but I want to reemphasize it again because of its importance. Having it all is going to cost you something. You may have to pay a price now to get something greater later. Some of you may already be paying a price right now and you don't have it all. Why not be in pursuit of something greater?

You may have to make some hard decisions, but I'm telling you that it will be worth it. The memories of those years of lack are some of my greatest because they brought me to this point in my life. And let me tell you something, I am literally living the best years of my life right now. My son is enjoying great success as a young entrepreneur, we are traveling the world together, we have multiple successful businesses, and we are healthier now than we have ever been.

I want to encourage you as you read this book today. The road may be rough right now, but it is going to get better. Trust me. It will get better. Sometimes it has to get worse before it gets better, but the promise is that it will get better.

Freedom is available to you. You can live life on your terms. I had to go through the darkest of valleys to come to a place of complete happiness and freedom. This is possible for you because the focus is not just on yachts, mansions, and luxurious cars. It is the freedom to live a fulfilled life that is completely balanced.

CHAPTER TEN

Let's Get Practical

N ow, my friends, I want to be clear about something with you. All of my experiences and difficulties motivated me to make a change in my life. However, and this is **IMPORTANT**, change would not have occurred without the practical action I put in place to ensure my success. You see, it's not enough just to be inspired and motivated if those emotions don't cause you to change. If you are looking for sheer motivation, then you will spend the rest of your life allowing your emotions to dictate your actions. And that is a frustrating road. Trust me, I've walked it before.

Like I said, when the doctor told my grandfather to, "change or die," I was moved at the time. I even thought about it after I left the hospital, but I returned to my life without making any of the necessary changes. Why? Because change is hard and it requires you to move outside of what makes you comfortable in order to achieve life transformation.

This is where it can become overwhelming because you may be thinking, "I don't even know where to start. I know some of what needs to be changed, but I don't know how to do it. What first step should I take?" These thoughts are actually really great. I had similar thoughts during my transition, so I decided to find people who had experienced what I had already gone through or who were achieving a level of success that I wanted to have.

There's a proverb that I live by that says, "Two are better than one because they have a good return for the work they have done. If one person falls, the other will be there to help him up. But what happens to the person who falls alone?" I love this saying because it embodies the way I live my life. I believe in investing in the lives of others and allowing others to invest in me. It is so essential that you get someone in your corner who is able to support you and assist you through every step of the process.

As a coach, speaker, and author, I have helped countless people achieve their desired success through my business, **Mentor with Maddix**, and it did not take years to accomplish. In fact, in most instances, dramatic life change occurred within weeks. I use a proven system that includes practical steps that will assist you in transforming your life. My son Caleb is also a speaker, CEO, entrepreneur and author who has dedicated his life to helping kids and teens through his business, Kids 4 Success.

Together, Caleb and I have been changing families through our hugely successful one on one coaching sessions that empower, inspire, and challenge. Below you will find a detailed description of what *Mentor with Maddix* entails. I encourage you to take your time reading through it and decide how serious you are about experiencing radical life change. If you are ready, then Caleb and I are awaiting your call with great anticipation. Our mission and purpose is about giving back and changing lives. Get us in your corner and we will give you all the tools and resources that have helped us have it all.

Mentor with Maddix:

If you want to have a closer relationship with your family as well as have the financial means to go on vacations without having to worry about a stressful budget, then you need to check out *Mentor With Maddix*!

Now I know that's a bold claim, as well as quite the cliffhanger and I promise I'll get back to it… but first:

A word of warning:

- If you don't believe there are any areas you can improve on as a parent

- If you ONLY care about your success and don't want to invest in your family's success

- If you don't prioritize integrity

- If you don't want to become a better parent

- If you don't love your kids

- If you are physically, emotionally or sexually abusive to your kids

- If you are unwilling to seek help and practice personal accountability

- If you could care less if your kids respect and trust you

- If you are not willing to admit your flaws and admit when you are wrong

This list can go on for a long, long time, but I think you can see the direction it's heading...

Anyway... If you fit ANY of the points on that obnoxiously long list, then DON'T even look into *Mentor With Maddix.*

In fact we don't want you here!

So if you're on that list, STOP READING NOW. You'll be wasting your time!

Now that we got that cleared up.

What is *Mentor With Maddix*?

Mentor with Maddix is an annual coaching and mentorship for success minded families with Caleb and I.

What you'll get:

A weekly Coaching Video from Caleb and I

Each and every week Caleb and I will send you a new video where we'll talk about things such as:

- "The 10 Habits of Happy Families"

- "How We Get So Much Done and Still Have Time to Enjoy Life and Have Fun"

- "The 10 Commandments of Every Happy Family"

- "Our Biggest Mistakes and The Lessons that we Learned from Them"

- "The 10 Secrets of Communication that Families can use to Avoid Misunderstanding and Fighting in the Home"

- "Routines, Traditions and Schedules of Very Successful Families"

- "The Top Seven Ways to a Stress Free Home and How to Have Peace and Harmony"

- "The Four Pillars of Our Home and How We Build Our Entire Life Around Them"

If you were to buy just the annual video training course this would cost you $1,997

A Weekly LIVE Q&A with Caleb for the Kids

Your kids can ask questions until their hearts content and all 52 Q&A sessions with Caleb will be recorded so your kids can watch them over again. Considering how busy he is, this is worth at LEAST $997

Caleb will talk to your kids about things such as:

- "Five Things That I Did Everyday That Helped Me Become Successful"

- "Why and How to Show Respect to your Parents even when you don't agree with them"

- "Why You Should Be Very Careful About The Type of Friends That You Hang Out With and How I Avoid Negative Friends"

Weekly LIVE Q&A with Me for all the parents out there.

You can ask as many questions as you like and again, all 52 Q&A sessions with me will be recorded. This is also a $997 value.

I will be answering question such as:

- "How you can Restore Broken Trust and Heal Pain You May Have Caused"

- "How to Empower and Motivate Your Kids Without Pushing Them too Hard"

- "The Top 10 Things that I Did To Help Train Caleb To Become What He Is Today"

Here's what it will do for your kids:

Every parent wants to hear good things about their children… that's exactly what *Mentor with Maddix* will do for you.

Your kids will begin to develop traits and qualities such as:

- Positive Attitude

- Honesty and Integrity

- Focused Mindset

- Discipline

- Kind and Giving

- Good Work Ethic

- Organized and Clean Room

- Good with Money

- Commitment to Reading Good Books

- Commitment to Daily Exercise and Eating Healthy

- Respect for Parents and Authority

- Better Manners

- Healthy Self-Esteem

- Strong Confidence

- Better Moods and Energy

I know we're all a little bit selfish, but don't worry… **_Mentor_** **_with Maddix_** isn't just for the kids. In fact it's just as much, if not more for the parents.

What *Mentor With Maddix* will do for YOU:

Now we get to the good stuff... how *Mentor With Maddix* will help you:

- You'll effortlessly have a more positive attitude

- You'll have a focused mindset that allows you to finish boring tasks quicker... say goodbye to a full day of chores and hello to a full episode of, "House of Cards"

- You'll be more disciplined which will make eating healthy a breeze

- You'll have unmatched work ethic that will take your business to the next level or get that new promotion you've been dying for

- Money will no longer be the master of you because you will be the master of it. You'll be on the way to financial freedom in no time

- Your kids will respect your authority

- You'll have healthy self-esteem

- You'll have strong confidence

- You'll be in better moods and have more energy than a little kid testing out their new sneakers by running in circles a few hundred times.

Look, *Mentor with Maddix* will make a bigger impact on your life than any life coach, or other coaching program could even dream of!

I know what you're thinking...

"Not ANOTHER coaching program!"

Caleb and I have a wonderful bond, financial freedom and a healthy lifestyle. In fact, that's the reason we are doing *Mentor with Maddix*. It is more than just a coaching program.

We want to share with you what we've learned together. We want to help you discover the secrets that we have uncovered that have transformed our lives.

Since our goal is to help families achieve physical, financial, spiritual and relational success, we want to give it to you for a price that is unheard of.

How much does it cost?

Even though there's $3,991 worth of content and coaching time in *Mentor with Maddix*...

We want to charge you even more because of the results we're getting!

Don't worry… I'm teasing you! But after that last statement, I'm glad you haven't closed this page, unfollowed us on social media and burned your computer.

In all honesty, I only said that to make you feel EVEN better about the real price, which is…

"Only $797"

Yes you read that correctly. You can get *Mentor With Maddix* for only $797

If you haven't achieved the level of success your striving for and you can't fork over $797 without thinking twice, then that's not a problem in the slightest!

So first off, we'll help get you there, and second off, if you aren't in the place to pay $797 here's what we want to do for you…

We want to give you *Mentor With Maddix* for only **$97** a month!

That's only $3.23 a day!

I looked up what else you can buy for $3.23. You wanna' know the best answer I found?

A Big Mac from McDonalds.

If you had to choose between that and your kids' and family's success, then you would have to be crazy to pick the Big Mac. So either you can buy a Big Mac with your $3.23, or you can make an investment in your family's future that is sure to pay you back 10 times over.

Which are you going to choose?

"Buy my family's future success for the price of a Big Mac? What's the catch?"

You know that ole' saying, "If it's too good to be true, then it probably is."

Well that's sorta' true even in this scenario. So here's the catch:

There are only 1,000 spots available!

So you NEED to hurry.

But it gets even better!

We want to make an impact on people. The easiest way we can do that is to get them into *Mentor With Maddix*. So to make this even more of a no brainer, when you sign up, we also want to throw in…

3 unbelievable BONUSES!!!

Bonus 1: Free membership to MyHealth90

MyHealth90 is a 90-day program that focuses on key health habits that will transform your life. Each person that finishes the program loses an average of 40lbs. If you are trying to improve your overall health or are in need of shedding a few pounds, this program will provide the tools you need in order to succeed. If you were to sign up for MyHealth90 right now it would cost you, $497.

Bonus 2: Monthly Book from Caleb and I

The same type of content you know and love is now in book format each and every month... enough said! You will have 12 books that Caleb and I have written together that are specifically focused on family.

We thought about selling this alone for $249, but they are yours for free when you sign up for *Mentor With Maddix.*

Bonus 3: Free Annual Membership to Kids 4 Success for your kids

Kids 4 Success is Caleb and Emily Shai's company where they help kids set and reach goals. (Emily is 11 years old and she wrote her own book and made over $20,000 selling it)

Your kids will get:

- A monthly group call with Caleb and Emily

- A weekly coaching video from Caleb and Emily

- A Kids 4 Success notebook

- And Premium access to the Kids 4 Success Page for K4S celebrities only

  The total value of Kids 4 Success is valued at $3,349. You obviously aren't going to be paying this much because we are giving it to you for free, but it would be worth every penny. Many of the kids involved in this program are waking up earlier, writing their own books, getting better grades and starting their own businesses

As a parent, seeing your kids become successful is priceless... but we put a price on it... FREE! All you need to do is sign up for *Mentor with Maddix*.

These bonuses alone are worth $4,095 but we are going to give them to you for free when you sign up for *Mentor with Maddix*

The total value for *Mentor with Maddix* including bonuses is, $8,086

But if you act right now you can get EVERYTHING for only one upfront payment of **$797** or a monthly payment of **$97**... which is only $3.23 a day!

Here's what I want you to do now

Go to mentorwithmaddix.com to fill out your information in 93 seconds or less and you'll get instant access to *Mentor with Maddix*, Kids 4 Success, MyHealth90 and a monthly book from Caleb and I.

I hate the silly false scarcity thing so I'm going to be very transparent with you. There's really no reason we are allowing 1,000 families into *Mentor with Maddix* except that it is the quickest way to get people into the program and therefore serve more families and eliminate the procrastinators and those who are not truly committed to their family.

Yeah, we like to keep it real with you guys so we don't lose your trust. ;)

So here comes some more manufactured scarcity, this book is going out to millions of interested buyers and as soon the 1,000 spots are filled, that's it!

So you really need to hurry. In fact, spots are filling up as we speak. If you don't go to **mentorwithmaddix.com** to sign up you'll miss out on this offer forever and be stuck eating Big Macs for the rest of your life.

WWW.MENTORWITHMADDIX.COM

Made in the USA
Columbia, SC
06 October 2017